From:

Mom, what I want you to know:

Published by Sourcebooks, Inc.
P.O. Box 4410, Naperville, Illinois 60567-4410
(630) 961-3900
Fax: (630) 961-2168
www.sourcebooks.com

ISBN-13: 978-1-4022-0813-3
ISBN-10: 1-4022-0813-8

Printed and bound in China
LEO 10 9 8 7 6 5 4 3 2 1

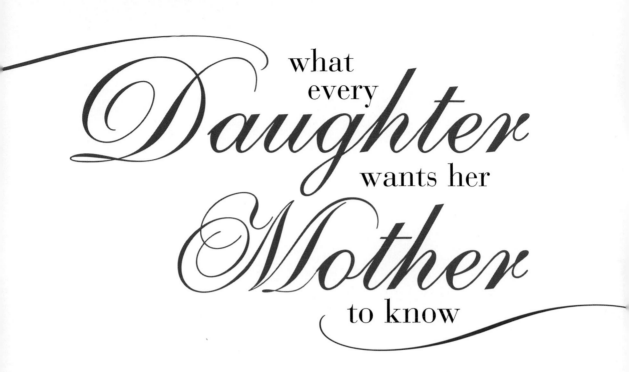

what
every
Daughter
wants her
Mother
to know

*...from the heart about love, life and
what you've taught me*

BETTY KELLY SARGENT & BETSY F. PERRY

SOURCEBOOKS, INC.®
NAPERVILLE, ILLINOIS

To my daughter Caroline Loomis,
who taught me how to listen.

—B. Perry

To my daughter Elizabeth Lee Kelly,
who taught me how to love.

—B. Sargent

Introduction

Every woman is a daughter, and there is probably no bond in nature stronger than that between mothers and daughters. We love each other, we hate each other, we support each other, and through it all, the impact we have on each other's lives is enormous. We all have a primal need to be loved and appreciated by our mother. A mother's warmth and acceptance, or lack of it, probably does more to shape her daughter's life than anything else. "Because our mothers are our first and most powerful female role models, our most deeply imagined beliefs about ourselves as women come from them," says Dr. Christiane Northrup.

The mother-daughter relationship is not always smooth, but it is always profound. How often do we hear women say, "I owe everything I am to my mom's love and understanding"? Or, conversely "If only my mother had been able to listen to me, to accept me as I really am instead of always wanting me to be more like her, my life could have been so different."

One woman named Sally told us about the fight she'd had with her mother when she was only five. Sally had desperately wanted panties with ruffles and patent-leather shoes with no straps, but her mother flatly refused. She remembers lying down on the sidewalk and crying hysterically because mom wouldn't even begin to explain why she couldn't have those shoes and panties. Instead, her mom stormed off in a huff saying, "I have no idea how to handle you," and that was the beginning of a lifetime of misunderstandings between Sally and her mother. All she had wanted was for her mother to hear her—to try, just a little, to understand the feelings behind her request. But her mother didn't know how to listen to her, and she certainly wasn't able to understand that there was a lot more to this tantrum than the need for grown-up Mary Janes and fancy panties.

"Because of the way my mother dealt with me, I just wasn't trained to listen," Sally said, "and now, years later, I'm trying to make things right with my own daughter. I make a real effort not to prejudge, to listen carefully to what she's asking, to try to understand what she is feeling, and to be supportive even when I completely disagree with her point of view. This hasn't been easy, but I know that making the effort to be sensitive to what she is really saying has helped me become a better mom than my own mother was for me."

Elaine has a different story to tell. Remarkably, she always felt so loved and appreciated by her mother that even when she was going through a horrendous divorce in her forties she never once doubted herself or her ability to handle whatever life dished out. "My mother's love was like a protective shield," she said. "Mom made me feel so smart and strong and competent, even when I grew up and noticed that I was twenty pounds overweight and that a lot of women were prettier, richer, and more successful than I was, it just didn't matter. I've never felt alone or insecure as an adult because my mother convinced me that I was the brightest, nicest, best little girl in the world, and I knew my mom would never lie."

We asked hundreds of young and not-so-young women to look into their hearts and tell us about all those feelings they were never able to express to their mothers. What we found was an outpouring of love and longing, of pain and tenderness.

Whether our mothers were affectionate and accepting, erratic and critical, or some combination of the two, the fact is that much of who we are today springs from our relationship with our mothers. Our mothers are contained in us just as we are, or were, contained in them. It is only by recognizing the influence our mothers had upon us that we can put it in its proper perspective and free ourselves to become healthy, loving, independent, adult women.

In speaking with hundreds of daughters about their feelings for their moms, we were surprised to hear how often women felt there were so many things they wish they had been able to say to their mothers—so many emotions, both positive and not-so-positive, that they wish they had been able to express. Even for many of the daughters who are still living at home, or whose mothers are right down the street, there were often great gaps between what the daughters were feeling and what they were actually able to say to their mothers.

Every mother is also a daughter, and often it is not until the daughter becomes a mother herself that she is able to see her relationship with her own mother in a new light. This is a book for us, for all of us daughters, whatever our age, whatever our relationship with our mother, whether our mother is still living or not. This book is a celebration of motherhood and daughterhood in all its richness and complexity. It is meant to touch the hearts of mothers and daughters everywhere.

"Biology is the least of what makes someone a mother."

—OPRAH WINFREY

Mom, I've always wanted you to know...

Even though I look like I'm not listening,
your voice is the first one I hear.

You are the best Mom...

I'm sorry I made fun of you that time you danced around the table and sang along to the Rolling Stones on the radio.

Mom, I've always wanted you to know...

You are the one person
I really, really *trust*.

Mom, I've always wanted you to know...

My favorite thing
growing up was coming home from school and
knowing you'd drop everything to hear about
my day even though you were probably bored to
tears with my endless stories about who'd been
mean to me that day.

"I take a very practical view of raising children. I put a sign in each of their rooms: check-out time is eighteen years."

—ERMA BOMBECK

Mom, I know you want the best for me...

It took me years to realize that when you told me I looked tired or that my hair was dirty, you did it out of *love,* not criticism.

Mom, I've always wanted you to know...

A hug is really a hug
when you *squeeze*.

Mom, I've always wanted you to know…

Sometimes you wonder why I raise my voice when we're talking. Simple—I need to make sure you're *hearing me.*

Mom, I've always wanted you to know...

Your *approval* means the world to me,
so please don't underestimate how much
I suffer from your disapproval.

"Every beetle is a gazelle
in the eyes of its Mother."

—Moorish Proverb

Mom, I've always wanted you to know...

Even in those times when the going got tough for you, I always felt how much you

loved me.

You are the best Mom...

Now that I'm a *grown-up* I'd rather
not think of you so much as a Mother,
but more as a consultant.

Mom, I've always wanted you to know . . .

You have always been the bank where I deposit
all my *fears*
and disappointments.

Mom, I've always wanted you to know...

When I was in school I used to be jealous
because you were so popular with my friends.

Now I'm proud.

"Generation after generation of women have pledged to raise their daughters differently, only to find that their daughters grow up and fervently pledge the same thing."

—Elizabeth Debold

Mom, I've always wanted you to know...

I love it when you are *proud* of me.

You are the best Mom…

It is great that you are so independent,
but when you occasionally ask for help
I just love it. It makes me feel
that you still need me, just as

I need you.

Mom, I know you want the best for me . . .

I know my lifestyle may not be exactly
what you hoped for,
but I really appreciate the fact that you never
bug me about it.

Mom, I know you want the best for me...

Just knowing you are always there for me makes
me feel totally (well, almost totally)
safe and secure.

"Making the decision to have a child
is momentous. It is to decide forever
to have your heart go walking around
outside your body."

—Elizabeth Stone

You are the best Mom…

Even when I was little, you always
respected my dignity.
Now I'm able to do that with others.

Mom, I've always wanted you to know…

It was your daily phone call that
absolutely saved my life the first time
I had *my heart broken*.

You are the best Mom...

The greatest gift you gave me was
the permission to be myself.

Mom, I've always wanted you to know...

It wasn't until I had a child of my own that I appreciated how truly *exceptional* you are.

"Neurotics build castles in the air; psychotics live in them. My mother cleans them."

—Rita Rudner

Mom, I know you want the best for me . . .

I know you'll always give me good *advice,*
even if it makes me squirm while you're doing it.

Mom, I've always wanted you to know...

It always surprises me when I hear *your* *words* come out of my mouth.

You are the best Mom…

I know you love me with *all your heart*.
I hope you love yourself enough.

Mom, I know you want the best for me...

Father knows best, but Mom knows *everything.*

"Women's Liberation is just a lot of foolishness. It's the men who are discriminated against. They can't bear children. And no one's likely to do anything about that."

—Golda Meir

You are the best Mom…

You always had an uncanny ability to *understand* what I was unable to say.

Mom, I've always wanted you to know...

I'll never forget that time when I was crying because I'd gotten my first pair of glasses and I thought I looked awful. You said I looked "extremely sophisticated." At five, I had no idea what that meant, but it
made me feel wonderful.

Mom, I know you want the best for me...

I'll never forget the *hug* that you gave me
and the tears in your eyes when I left home
for the first time.

You are the best Mom...

When it finally occurred to me that you are just
a big *little girl,* I loved you all the more.

"Any Mother could perform the jobs of several air traffic controllers with ease."

—LISA ALTHER

Mom, I've always wanted you to know...

I love that you refer to my dogs
as your *granddogs*.

Mom, I've always wanted you to know...

By the time I realized that maybe *you were right,* I had kids of my own who were positive that everything I did was wrong.

Mom, I've always wanted you to know...

I hope you realize that I accept you for who you are, and I know that you always did *the best you could.*

Mom, I know you want the best for me...

You taught me there are three ways
to get something done:
1. Hire someone to do it
2. Do it myself
3. Forbid my kids to do it
It works!

"A Mother's children are portraits of herself."

—UNKNOWN

Mom, I know you want the best for me...

When at first I don't succeed, I try doing what
you told me to do in the first place.

Mom, I've always wanted you to know…

Nothing makes me happier than *your praise*.
Nothing hurts more than your criticism,
even when you don't mean it as criticism.
Please try to remember how much I value
your input, and that, in the end,
only I can change myself.

You are the best Mom…

I may not always like you, but
I always *love you*.

You are the best Mom...

I like to think that every *confidence* I share
with you will always be our secret.

"Most of all the other beautiful things in life come by twos and threes, by dozens and hundreds. Plenty of roses, stars, sunsets, rainbows, brothers and sisters, aunts and cousins, comrades, and friends—but only one Mother in the whole wide world."

—Kate Douglas Wiggin

You are the best Mom...

I've always respected your right to lie about your age. But now that you are younger than I am, it might be time for us to rethink this.

Mom, I've always wanted you to know...

When I finally realized that I was going
to be just like you when I grew up,
it actually made me *happy!*

You are the best Mom...

I feel myself becoming more *like you* every day.

Mom, I've always wanted you to know…

Mom, I worry I won't be as *good* a mother as you were.

"Grown don't mean nothing to a mother. A child is a child. They get bigger, older, but grown? What's that supposed to mean? In my heart it don't mean a thing."

—Toni Morrison

Mom, I've always wanted you to know...

Because you were such
a *wise and patient* mother,
I've learned how to mother myself.

Mom, I've always wanted you to know…

I think you should know that
I did peek at the Christmas presents you
thought you'd hidden so well.

Mom, I know you want the best for me…

I hope you know how *extraordinary* you really are, and you'll never settle for second best.

Mom, I know you want the best for me…

It finally occurred to me that
maybe you weren't the only difficult person in
our *relationship*.

"My mother used to say 'he who angers you, conquers you!' But my mother was a saint."

—Elizabeth Kenney

"Women know the way to rear up children (to be just). They know a simple, merry knack of tying sashes, fitting baby shoes, and stringing pretty words that make no sense, and kissing full sense into empty words."

—Elizabeth Barrett Browning

"With my poems, I finally won even my mother. The longest wooing of my life."

—MARGE PIERCY

"When I stopped seeing my mother with the eyes of a child, I saw the woman who helped me give birth to myself."

—NANCY FRIDAY

"I cannot forget my mother. She is my bridge. When I needed to get across, she steadied herself long enough for me to run across safely."

—RINITA WILLIAMS

"There's a lot more to being a woman than being a mother, but there's a hell of a lot more to being a mother than most people suspect."

—Roseanne Barr

"This is part of the essence of motherhood, watching your kid grow into her own person and not being able to do anything about it. Otherwise children would be nothing more than pets."

—HEATHER ARMSTRONG

"The world is full of women blindsided by the unceasing demands of motherhood, still flabbergasted by how a job can be terrific and torturous."

—ANNA QUINDLEN

"Being a full-time mother is
one of the highest salaried jobs in my field,
since the payment is pure love."

—Mildred B. Vermont

"When you are a mother, you are never really alone in your thoughts. A mother always has to think twice: once for herself and once for her child."

—Sophia Loren

"Motherhood has a very humanizing effect.
Everything gets reduced to essentials."

—MERYL STREEP

Mom, I know you want the best for me...

Can you please not make
that scrunched up
"I told you so" face when I admit
to having made a mistake?

Mom, I know you want the best for me…

Even though I sometimes resist *your* *advice,* I always take it very seriously.

"A mother is a person who, seeing there are only four pieces of pie for five people, promptly announces she never did care for pie."

—Tenneva Jordan

"Food, love, career, and mothers:
the four major guilt groups."

—CATHY GUISEWITE

"A mother is not a person to lean on,
but a person to make leaning unnecessary."

—Dorothy Canfield Fisher

Mom, I know you want the best for me . . .

Mom, stop pressuring me to get married.
I need time to figure out what role men will play
in my life and how to relate to them before
I make a trip down the aisle.
Please stop nudging me into matrimony.

Mom, I've always wanted you to know…

Sometimes I think you don't understand that
I can love you very much, but still need
to be free to lead my own life and make
my own mistakes.

You are the best Mom…

I am who I want to be because you were
who you wanted to be.

Mom, I know you want the best for me…

I know you don't believe this, but Mom, *we have different tastes.* I don't want pink shoes, a headband, or anything peach in my closet. If you respect my taste, I promise not to buy you any more low-rise jeans.

"I thought about all of us women and how we spend half our lives rebelling against our mothers and the next half rebelling against our daughters."

—Lois Wise

Mom, I've always wanted you to know...

My *greatest fear* is recognizing you in myself. My *greatest joy* is recognizing you in myself.

You are the best Mom…

You taught me that we are all *responsible* for our own happiness. When I finally stopped blaming other people, everything started to change for the better.

"God could not be everywhere,
so he created mothers."

—JEWISH PROVERB

"What a child doesn't receive, he can seldom later give."

—P.D. JAMES

Mom, I've always wanted you to know...

You are my hero.
I love you.

Acknowledgments

We'd like to thank the hundreds of women all over the country who took the time and effort to search their hearts and share with us their deepest thoughts and feelings about their mothers. We are so grateful for your honesty, openness, and candor.

Thank you all.

About the Authors

BETTY KELLY SARGENT

Betty Sargent, a veteran book and magazine editor, has been editor-in-chief of William Morrow, executive editor-at-large for HarperCollins, and book and fiction editor for *Cosmopolitan* magazine—where she also did biweekly book reviews on Sunday mornings for CNN. Her most recent book is *Beautiful Bones without Hormones*, with Leon Root, MD. She is the mother of a daughter and son, neither of whom have registered any major complaints so far.

BETSY F. PERRY

Betsy Perry runs the New York office of the Milken Institute. Previously she was the global news event producer and a branding strategist for Bloomberg LP. Prior to that she was a producer at Fox Broadcasting and a senior editor at *Cosmopolitan* magazine. She is the mother of one daughter in her late twenties and they chat on the phone almost every day.